# BE A SUCCESSFUL AFFILIATE MARKETER

# BY STEPHEN AKINTAYO

# TABLE OF CONTENT

# CHAPTER ONE

# INTRODUCTION TO AFFILIATE MARKETING

# CHAPTER ONE
## *Introduction*

Congratulations buddy.
I see you have decided to try out affiliate marketing, that's all well and good.

Without an iota of doubt, I can confidently tell you that Affiliate Marketing is one of the quickest and easiest way to earn income on the internet.

Apart from earning income online, other benefits that come with affiliate marketing include:

• Zero to very minimum financial investment to start out with in Affiliate Marketing

• A wide variety of Affiliate Marketing programs to choose from;

• Commission schemes that range from 20% to as high as 90% of the selling price

• Ability to earn income as result is being productive without any restriction by time

• Earn without limits and work at your own pace.

As a result of these numerous benefits, millions of internet users have tried their hands in affiliate marketing, but I want to assure you right now that with the help of this guide you are reading, you are guaranteed to succeed in this path even if you are a first timer.

How?

By studying every line of this manual you are reading right now and following every instruction there in to the latter as follow:

1. Choose a subject.

2. Look for a good affiliate program to subscribe to.

3. Create your own website.

4. Create a Unique Selling Proposition for your product.

5. Create and distribute a product that is capable of going viral.

6. Write and distribute articles on different platforms.

7. Start an email marketing campaign.

*AFFILIATE MARKETING CYCLE*

This doesn't have to be a complicated process at all. Making money online via affiliate marketing is one of the easiest ways online.

In this manual, you will be exposed to simplify affiliate marketing with practical techniques that you can actually adopt to make promoting your product a success

Now let us take a look at the seven steps highlighted above one after the other closely in each of the chapters.

# CHAPTER TWO

# CHOOSE A SUBJECT

# CHAPTER TWO
## *Choose A Subject*

First and foremost, you should try to pinpoint a subject that you have passion for. That way, it is with ease that you will be able to write about something that you are actually interested in. Imagine choosing to write about cooking when you don't even like cooking? How will you fare in such a venture? Without the love and the passion for your subject matter, it will never be able to push it to its full potential. Also, you'll easily get bored with it. And once you get bored, it becomes hard work maintaining your business online.

Endeavour to find a subject matter that you love, or at the very least, a topic that you like. There are many fields that one can focus on. You like animals? Maybe you can consider the broader subject of pets, or picking a more specific breed of an animal. Or better still, focus on a more particular branch, like animal health or care.

Choose a Subject

Your choice of market will depend on a couple of factors which include:

• How well you know the said market? Passion will bring you a lot of benefits, so might as well choose a market that you are passionate about from the very beginning.

• How interested are you in the said market? Knowledge is an ongoing commitment. You have to constantly keep yourself updated so as not to get left behind with the latest trends and tactics in your industry. Might as well choose a market that you are interested in, to make the constant search for knowledge more enjoyable and fulfilling.

• What is the outlook for the said market? Naturally, you wouldn't want to focus on a dying market, where the products you are trying to sell for example have saturated the digital market. You will want to look for a hungry market, one which will be able to sustain profitability for a long time. This brings us to the next question

• How big is the demand of the said market? This is the first component of economic success which states that demand should be high.

• What is the size of the competition in the said market? This is the second component of economic success where it is expected that supply should be low.

High Demand + Low supply = Profitable market

This is the ONE FORMULA you should remember whenever you are ready to choose a market. It's the basic rule of economic success. It's the secret of so many high-profit businesses right from ages past up until now.

There are many online tools that you can use to determine the variables at play with the formula above.

There are websites you can visit to determine the demand of the said subject you want to discuss about.

Type in a subject you have in mind. You will then be taken to a page where a number of keywords and key phrases are suggested, together with the number of times they have been searched for in the search engines. You will want to choose subjects with high numbers of searches.

Now, finding a sub-topic that commands many searches is not enough. You need to determine how many websites are catering to it, since you'll be operating on the Internet. Run a search of the sub-topic at www.google.com. Look at the number of web pages that appear, as indicated on the top area of the results page.

If the subject commands 1,000,000 searches per month and there are 2,000,000 websites catering to the it, then the supply outweighs the demand and the chances of succeeding as an affiliate in such a field will be slimmer.

But if the subject commands 1,000,000 searches per month and there are only 2,000 websites catering to it, then you have for yourself a goldmine!
This is how you find a fertile market on the World Wide Web.

# CHAPTER THREE

# CHOOSE AN AFFILIATE PROGRAM

## CHAPTER THREE
### *Choose an Affiliate Program*

Once you have been able to determine a market you want to cater to, it's time to now choose a suitable affiliate program for the market.

There are two choices here:
1. Either you choose an affiliate program; or
2. You join an affiliate network

Let's take a closer look at each of them.
An *affiliate network* is one where the merchant directly employs an affiliate system to hire affiliates. The affiliates deal with the merchant directly. There is no third party involved. The merchant will be the one to distribute affiliate links, give away items to help in promoting the products, and ultimately, pay the affiliates their commissions.

An *affiliate network*, on the other hand, is a system which an affiliate can join. Upon enrollment, he will gain access to hundreds, if not thousands, of products from different merchants. He can decide which product to promote. The affiliate network serves as the middleman between the affiliates and the merchants. There are pros and cons for each choice.

An affiliate network is an excellent choice for people who can't decide on what product to promote. With the myriad of choices presented by affiliate networks, and with the freewill to choose any product at any time, affiliate networks offer great opportunities for would-be affiliate marketers.

The cons?

Thousands, if not millions, of people share the same thought about affiliate networks. This means thousands, if not millions, of competitors for you for any product you will choose under a particular affiliate network. The secret to online success is actually quite simple. It can be summarized through the equation below...

High demand for a product + few competition = maximum profit
This equation holds for any business.
Affiliate networks may offer a hot product, but if millions of affiliates will promote it, your chances of succeeding will be greatly reduced.

However, this doesn't mean that you can't succeed if you're enrolled under an affiliate network. With the succeeding lessons, you will learn how to up your game and emerge victorious in the field of affiliate marketing even if you will be competing against millions of other affiliates.

Now, on to *affiliate programs*...

An *affiliate program*, will usually offer fewer products for you to promote. You'll be limited to the merchant's products only.

However, affiliate programs employ fewer affiliates which means less competition. And this further means greater chances to succeed. Not satisfied with the sales rate of a particular product under an affiliate program?

No probs!

You can join multiple affiliate programs! There is no limit as to how many affiliate programs you can join.

Better yet, almost all affiliate programs are free to join. They won't charge you a single kobo for your membership. After all, you are the one who will be helping the merchant sell his products. You are the one who has to be paid!

HOW AFFILIATE MARKETING WORKS

Now, there are good affiliate programs and there are bad affiliate programs.

How do you know which to avoid?

Be on the lookout for the following signs:

• Offering a product that is of inferior quality. This product may fill up a need somewhere, but because of its poor quality, refund requests will pour in. You may be able to refer some sales, but the refunds will take away your commission. Worse still, you might lose credibility amongst your prospects for leading them to a bad product.

• Offering a product that is difficult to sell. This is self-explanatory.
You won't be able to realize your commissions if the product you're tasked to pre-sell is a "hard sell."

• The affiliate program has a history of failing to pay its affiliates. Nothing is more frustrating than working for something but being deprived of the rewards for some reason or another.

• The affiliate program sometimes struggle when it comes to its finances.

• The affiliate program is being operated by a person or persons who are quite hesitant to introduce themselves most of the time.

If you see an affiliate program with any of these characteristics, run the other way.
Now, how do you determine the right affiliate program?

Basically, the right affiliate program should possess most, if not all, of the following characteristics:

• A hot-selling product. Personally, this is my number one concern. I will not be able to earn as an affiliate if I cannot pre-sell any products, right? Hence, I always look for programs offering products that have a proven value in a particular market, or at the very least, products which offer a lot of promise.

• Gratuitous commission scheme. This is next to the factor above

• A program that is well known for its credibility. Of course no one would want to associate themselves with flash in the pan, fly-by-night establishments, right? You want to be a winner? Stick with a winner! You will need to rely on recommendations and your own exercise of due diligence to find such an affiliate program will also eventually pay off.

• A program that has an excellent post-sales service. In affiliate marketing, refund request is something you want to try as much as possible to avoid.

You may be led to believe that you have bagged a sale, but if a refund is requested later on by the buyer, you end up not getting any commission. A program that has excellent post-sales support will be able to minimize any such requests, and consequently, will be able to protect your interests as far as your commission is concerned.

Examples of companies that offer affiliate programs in Nigeria include ecommerce websites such as Konga, Dealdey, Jumia, Business directories like Vconnect, Travel

agencies like wakanow and Virgin Atlantic etc. So what are you waiting for?
Start hunting!

# CHAPTER FOUR

# CREATE A WEBSITE

# CHAPTER FOUR
## *Create A Website*

World Wide Web

Some Internet marketing gurus will tell you that you can pursue affiliate marketing even without having a website. That's true.

However, having your own website will make things easier, and will multiply your profit tremendously.

A website is your headquarters in the cyberspace. If real life businesses have their brick and mortar stores, your affiliate marketing business will have a website as its virtual office. This is the value of having your own website, in a nutshell: a place that will be identified with your business, a central place where you can direct people so that they'll be exposed to your business message.

As an affiliate marketer, you can use your website to host all of your affiliate links. Now, why is this important?

Because as an affiliate, you will be given an affiliate link per product. Your prospects should click on your specific affiliate link so that any purchases they make will be credited under your account.

Affiliate links are what tells the affiliate system which commission goes to whom. Since you will be dealing with hundreds of products, you will have an equal amount of affiliate links. This can be quite tricky. If you're going to promote them individually, each affiliate link will require its own campaign.

But if you have your own website, you can have one main campaign to lead your prospects to your headquarters where all your affiliate links can be found. Everything will be centralized. Everything will be easier.

When you have decided to build your own website, you will need two things:

1. Domain name
2. Subscription to a web hosting service

Your domain name is your address on the World Wide Web. The URL www.Smehouse.com has "Smehouse" as its domain name.

When choosing a domain name for your affiliate marketing campaign, please bear in mind the following guidelines:

• The domain name should be relevant to the field you are engaged in.

• The domain name should be easy to remember.

• The domain name should be catchy.
• As much as possible, choose the extension ".com". You will also need a web hosting service.

Basically, you should be looking for 3 things from the web hosting service you are considering. These are:

1. Storage space – or how many files you can store in your account.

2. Bandwidth limit – or how much data transfer can be accommodated by the web hosting service. Do not settle for anything less than 15GB per month.

3. Excellent technical support – your website is your business partner. You will want it to be live all the time. In the event that it's down, the web hosting service should provide immediate assistance to bring it back up, as your business relies on it.

You will also need an autoresponder service. One thing which is of utmost importance, which we will discuss in detail in a latter step is email marketing.

Basically, much of your success will depend on how big and how responsive your mailing list will be. What's that? "Mailing list?" you may ask?

Indeed, you will have to build a mailing list to convert casual onlookers into leads. Your sales will come from your leads, after all.

And what makes email marketing possible is a subscription to an autoresponder service.

So it is important that you choose a fantastic autoresponder service to give you solid ground to stand on. Knowing all of this, creating a website should be easy.

For a website (and other digital marketing services), you can visit gtext.com.ng to have one created for you at a very affordable price.

*Why should people buy from you and not from others.*

Earlier, I told you that we will be discussing a technique that will greatly help you compete against thousands of affiliates promoting the same product. We will be tackling that right now. Answer me this...

Why should people buy from you instead of buying from others who are promoting the same product? Surely, your offer must have something special, something unique, something fabulous that will separate it from the rest.

This distinguishing factor is what we call the unique selling proposition or USP.
The USP, plain and simple, is the secret of the Internet marketing millionaires. Somehow, they have formulated a unique selling proposition that made the members of their target market take notice and compelled them to buy from the said successful NETREPRENEURS.

So I'll dare say this...Your affiliate marketing success will greatly depend on the potency of the USP you will be able to come up with. The USP states that you should be able to personalize an offer to make it better than the rest. Hence, you may be selling the same product to the same market, but if you can add something that will make your offer better, you'd naturally stand out amongst your competitors. People will notice you more and they will buy from you instead of buying from others.

In short... the USP is tantamount to putting your own twist into things. Take for example an affiliate program offering an eBook on wedding speeches. There are 1,000 affiliates promoting it, with you being one of them. The eBook sells for #1000, and commission is pegged at 50%, or #500 per sale. Now, how can you successfully make people click on your affiliate link instead of other's links? Add something that will make your offer more valuable.

There are countless, countless ways by which you can accomplish this. The limit is really your imagination. Let those creative juices flow and see for yourself how far this tactic can take you. One of the most popular USP applications is the act of adding bonuses to the offer. If you have other products that you would like to give away to people who order through your affiliate link, then announce it immediately. This will add to the value of your offer. When compared with the bare offers of other affiliates, yours will truly shine.

People will order from you. People will thank you for putting up a wonderful package. And people will trust you enough to order from you again.

There are many sources for the bonuses you can include. Let's take a look at some of them:

• Products which you have created yourself. Want some ideas? Do refer to the Information Product Creation Manual for some fantastic ideas.

• Products which you have caused the creation of. These are products you have asked a freelancer to create, and all the rights of which have accrued to you upon completion of the transaction. Want to protect your interests when it comes to your dealings with freelancers? Do refer to the Outsourcing Survival Kit, the first eBook on the matter of digital contracting of tasks for a fee.

• Products which you acquired with their master resale rights or private label rights. Knowing the different kinds of rights is a must in doing online business. Arm yourself with the right knowledge by reading All Rights Explained, the definitive tome for such a subject.

• Joint ventures. Others may already have fantastic products which will perfectly complement your offer.
Want more ideas?

Okay, so let's say you're in a mall, and you're looking for some new clothes to wear. One shop's offering a nice pair of pants for #10,000. Another shop is offering the same pair at a highly discounted rate of #9,000. What shop will you choose?

You'd naturally buy from the one which is offering a big discount, right?
The same goes in affiliate marketing. If you can offer the products you are pre-selling at a lower Price, then you'd be able to win over more prospects.

Wait. I know you're probably thinking…"But they're not my products. I don't set the price. How I offer discounts?"

Indeed, the price for the products you will pre-sell are more or less fixed by the affiliate merchants, but this shouldn't mean that you cannot offer discounts for them.

Where will the discounts come from? From your prospective commissions, of course. Suppose an eBook is being sold for #1,000, with the commission rate pegged at 50%, or #500 per sale. You can offer the same eBook for #900, and take away the #100 from the commission that will eventually be sent into your account.

Quite a number of affiliate merchants recognize this tactic, and they are willing to enter into a special arrangement with you. If not, you can always offer a cash rebate to the people who order through your link. You can promise them a certain percentage of the money back once you receive your commission from the affiliate merchant.

Yet another derivative of this tactic is offering discounts for future purchases. By that time, you will have received your commissions which shall answer the discounts you will offer.

Yes, this technique will cut down on your profit. But with the competitive nature of this field, it is an essential sacrifice. One step backwards, two steps forward, so they say. The rewards you will gain will make such a sacrifice very much worth it at the end of the day.

What we have enumerated above are just some of the more popular USP implementations today. They are tried and tested tactics that are being employed by the top affiliates of today. But you are not limited to them only. You can come up with a USP of your own. You can add your own personal touch on your offers to make them totally different and totally special. Then, you'd be able to capture the interest of the members of your market, and such is the start of a fruitful affiliate marketing campaign for you.

# CHAPTER FIVE

# CREATE VIRAL PRODUCT(S)

# CHAPTER FIVE
## *Create Viral Product(s)*

Armed with your affiliate links as well as your USP, you are ready to announce to the world your entry into the playing field. Here's a great tactic that you can employ for every major product launch that you promote.

Create a viral product

What's a viral product?
Basically, a viral product is a digital product, capable of being distributed digitally, that is of outstanding value. This digital product will promotes your affiliate link. It can be a timely eBook or special report, the pages of which will contain your affiliate link. It can be a software program where your affiliate link will appear in the user interface. Now, here's the clincher. You distribute the viral product for free. Yes, for FREE.

A product of high value, distributed for free! What's my purpose for that you would ask? What results do I expect? Well, suppose you receive something valuable, for free, wouldn't you feel special? Wouldn't you feel lucky? Wouldn't you feel happy? Wouldn't you want to share such feeling with   closest friends? You family members? The people you chat with in your favorite online forum? This is why it's called a "viral" product... because like a "virus," it spreads quite quickly, at an exponential rate at that.

What if every person who gets to enjoy my viral product refers it to 5 of his/her friends? 1 prospect can quickly become 5 prospects. 5 prospects can quickly become 25 prospects. 25 prospects can quickly become 125 prospects. And so on and so forth.

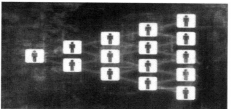

It can become a juggernaut of a cycle for the first few days. And often, such lasts for many, many months, if not years. Creating a viral product is actually easy.

Ask yourself, what are you good at? If you can create software programs, create software programs. If you can write, write eBooks and special reports. If you have a flair for videos or broadcasting, create a video or audio product that can be downloaded.

If you can't do any of these, hire a freelancer from websites like www.elance.com, www.fiverr.com
and www.getafreelancer.com. Package the created product well and upload it to your website.

Yeah!

Promote the viral product on your landing page and the people who visit your website can download it. Just make sure that the following guidelines are observed:

1. Make sure to clearly remind your visitors that they can download the said product for free. People are generally hesitant to download anything on the World
Wide Web, believing that there is no such thing as a free lunch in the real and the online world.

2. Make sure to clearly remind the people who will download the said product that they are free to distribute it to other people. Sometimes, that reminding push goes a long, long way. The usage of a viral product is part and parcel of the powerful promotional strategy known as viral marketing. Viral marketing is basically word-of-mouth advertising in the virtual world. You want people to talk about the product you are promoting to generate that much needed hype.

Viral marketing has the following elements that are worth studying:
1. Viral marketing makes use of existing networks. There is no need to create your own web of contacts.

2. The business message must be easy to seed. It must be made apparent at the earliest stage. A convoluted message would just make the viral marketing campaign useless. If your business message, for example, is the promotion of your website's link, make pit appear conveniently and immediately.

3. The business message must circulate naturally. The goal is to reach as many people as possible. The means to achieve that goal is to promote persistent circulation of the business message. Circulation must be facilitated with minimal interference from the business owner. The message must replicate on its own. We should keep these in mind as we formulate a viral marketing plan.

4. You must have a value proposition. Let us illustrate this through an often used technique. Suppose your business offers a software package. How do you promote it through viral marketing? You could use the strategies suggested in the preceding sections to offer a free trial of your software for a certain period.

This is your value proposition. As more and more people get exposed to your software, they'll come to know of its worth and spread the word to their friends. Soon, after their trial period expires, they will have to order the full version.

This is your contingent proposition. From the latter, you will derive the profit to replace what you have spent in your initial investment. Once Return of Investment, or ROI, is achieved, everything else is your net profit, and you'll have lots of that as people will continue flocking to avail of your product, thanks to the exponential character of viral marketing.

5. You must have a contingent proposition. Do not lose sight of your bread and butter. The point to viral marketing is to sell your goods and services. Your goods and services are your contingent proposition.

Once your value proposition has lured the attention of your prospective clients, it is time to win them over to purchase your contingent proposition.

6. You should provide benefits for the participants. One thing that predominate

viral marketing campaigns is the constant use of the word "free." As many marketing resources have stated, the said word is probably the most powerful weapon to attract customers. Offering free goods or services to potential clients is an old and established rule in marketing, both offline and online to repay the kindness you have shown them.

Observing these principles of an effective viral marketing campaign will ensure a fruitful experience for your website

# CHAPTER SIX

# WRITING AND DISTRIBUTING

# CHAPTER SIX
## *Writing and Distributing*

In the previous step, we have discussed the efficiency of viral marketing once a prospect downloads your viral product from your website. But here's the deal...

You must first lead people to your website. How else can they find your viral product?

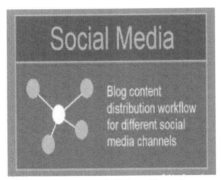

Writing and Distribution

Furthermore, even without the benefit of a viral product for download, people who are led to your website can still be exposed to your business message. They'll still be able to see your affiliate links. They can still be referred to the affiliate merchant's sales page. The best way to lead people to your website is through a process called article marketing.

Article marketing involves the submission of articles to as many article directories as possible. There is more to it than just that, of course. You might ask how a process which seems so simple could generate a lot of traffic for your website. That is a very valid question, but do consider the following benefits offered by article marketing.

• Article directories figure prominently well is SERPs. Hence, having your link displayed in the articles you submit would mean that your link will be exposed to the millions of visitors who visit the said article directories.

• Article directories have high PR. Having an article published, with an inbound link to your website, would give the latter a boost in its own public relation.
• If the article you submit is of excellent quality, it will have a good chance of getting picked up by webmasters. This means more

inbound links for you, and this will mean more visitors.

• There are so many article directories on the World Wide Web. Suppose you submit the same exact article to a hundred of them; that would mean a hundred inbound links guaranteed. But what if you submit ten or twenty articles? Again, traffic is a numbers game.

• Articles are low cost investments, and for most, they actually require no costs. This is an excellent option, considering that an article submitted to just one article directory could be generating traffic for your website for many years to come. Sold on article marketing yet? Here are the steps you should follow...

1. Pick a topic relevant to the subject of your website. As with our running example, if your website is dedicated to dog grooming, dog grooming tips or dog grooming items are good topics to discuss.

2. Research on your chosen topic. Try to discover something novel about it that hasn't been discussed to death in other channels.

3. Write an article that will share the information you have pinpointed.. Anything too short will not successfully convey what you want to convey. Anything too long would not sustain your readers' attention.

If you are not that confident about your writing prowess, or if you simply do not have the time to write an article, you could hire a freelancer to do the writing for you. However. Writing is one of those services where you get what you pay for most of the time. You can look for freelancers in places such as Fiverr.com. Don't proceed with this option blindly, however.

There are many risks to consider. I would suggest The Outsourcing Survival Kit which is the first of its kind to deal with all manners of digital outsourcing as well as the steps you should take to protect the interests of your business.

4. Include a resource box at the end of your article. Your resource box should contain a concise introduction of yourself and your business, as well as a link to your website.

5. Then, it would be time to submit your article to the many article directories on the World Wide Web. Remember to always include your resource box, because such will contain the link to your website.

Regarding the link you will use, well, you can choose either of 2 things:
1. The link to your website where all of your affiliate links are promoted; or
2. The particular affiliate link itself, although hidden via tools like *turbourl.com* People generally don't want to click on affiliate links.

# CHAPTER SEVEN

# IMPLEMENT AN EMAIL MARKETING SYSTEM

# CHAPTER SEVEN
## _Implement An Email Marketing System_

## Email Marketing

Here's a fact that every affiliate marketer should know

On the average, it takes 10 contacts with a prospect before he will decide to purchase what you are offering. What does this mean?

Well, if you manage to refer a person to the affiliate merchant's sales page the first time around, chances are, he won't buy whatever it is that's being offered. As a result, you won't win any commission. It will take 10 tries, on the average, before he will decide to make a purchase. The question, then, is this: How can you ensure that you will be able to contact your prospects at least 12 times?

The answer lies in a system called *email marketing*. Am email marketing system is also called a follow-up system because it enables you to "follow up" on your leads. Genius Internet marketers use a follow-up system to capture the contact details of their visitors so that they can somehow convince them to visit their websites again at a future time.

A follow-up system captures the email addresses of visitors and collects them in a subscription for a mailing list. The heart of every follow-up system is an excellent autoresponder service. An autoresponder service would allow you to prepare your messages beforehand and deliver them according to the schedule you will set. Additionally, an autoresponder service will also allow you to personalize your messages, well, automatically. Your recipients would be referred to by their given names, and in certain occasions, the autoresponder would even greet them on their birthdays. These, added to the act that an autoresponder service would take care of the subscriptions on auto-pilot, makes it an essential investment for every online business. But not all autoresponders are built alike.

Some are simply better than others. I would like to recommend *Formmule* service, which you will find in your google drive when you log into your google + account. This service is for free yet it delivers amazing results when used.

Once they have subscribed to your mailing list, you can start sending them emails with offers of your products. You can even inform them of updates to your website so that they may decide to check it out. How does this work, in actual practice?

You will be leading prospects to your website. Your website should have a capture device where your visitors can leave their email addresses. Their email addresses will thereafter be stored in your autoresponder, and the email marketing system will take care of the rest. The challenge lies in how you can make them leave their email addresses.

Once you have set up your autoresponder to handle your mailing list, you just have to come up with interesting offers to encourage your visitors to sign up for your list.

This can be done in a variety of exciting ways.
• You can offer free gifts to entice your visitors to subscribe to your list.
• You can offer to deliver a newsletter containing information about the subject they're interested in.
• You can conduct a contest, with their subscriptions as their raffle entries.
• You can offer access to other meatier portions of your website in exchange for their subscription.
• You can offer them discounts on your products if they'd join your mailing list.
There are, of course, more ways to bait your visitors into signing up to your mailing list. By employing a little creativity, you're sure to come up with innovative ways to lure visitors into your follow-up system.
In conclusion:
Form partnerships to increase your profit
There you have it.

Easy-to-follow steps to ensure your success in affiliate marketing!

But you don't have to stop there!
No!

You can always strive to increase your profit.
How?

Let's put it this way: two heads are always better than one. Two or more sets of resources are always better than one.

Two or more sets of prospects are always better than one. Earlier, we shared with you the secret to Internet marketing success:
High demand for a product + few competition = maximum profit

Now, let me let you in on the secret to success in this industry:

*Joint ventures*

Joint ventures are partnerships between two or more Internet marketers for the success of a particular campaign.

There are many benefits to this. First, it reduces incidental expenses. Second, it reduces the risks since there is an input of more ideas and the exercise of more checks. Third, in case of failure (which is rare,) it reduces the damage incurred as it shall be borne by more than one person. Needless to say, Joint ventures have become a very lucrative model for most online businesses.

As you become successful in affiliate marketing, always remember that your success shouldn't stop there. Affiliates rely on a continuous influx of leads. And you can generate more leads if you team up with other online businessmen.

I call Joint ventures brotherhoods. Your partners will be your brothers. You will care for each other. You will go out of your way for each other. And you will all enjoy the glory together.

You want SUSTAINABLE success...
Success that will last a long, long time.
This kind of success can be achieved via the right attitude, the right system, and the right amount of effort you invest. We wish you nothing but the best in your Affiliate Marketing Endeavors. Cheers!

SME House Resources.

ATTENTION!!!
You have downloaded this ebook because you wanted to increase your knowledge of how you can make money via the internet.
With just #25,000, you can get:

A customized bulk SMS website (Delivered within 24 hours)

Free SMS units to kick start your bulk SMS business

Free ebook on how to make 6-7 figure income monthly

Nationwide phone number database
3 Months free mentorship

This offer ends as soon as we reach 10 people and then the price goes back to #100,000 after the first 10 people pay.

Take advantage....Call Tobi Now on 08034568079

# Be a successful
# Affiliate Marketer

For information, please contact email: info@stephenakintayo.com
or
stephenakintayo@gmail.com
This publication is intended to provide accurate and authoritative information in regard to the subject matter covered.

It is sold with the understanding that the publisher is not engaged in rendering legal, accounting or other professional services.

If legal advice or other expert assistance is required, the services of a competent professional person should be sought.

Stephen Akintayo Is An Inspirational Speaker, Author, Youth Leader, And Entrepreneur.

A Digital Marketing Consultant With Various Multinationals In Nigeria, He Is Also The Publisher/Editor-In-Chief Of CEO PROTEGE MAGAZINE, A Business Magazine Published By CEOPROTEGE LIMITED.

He Is Presently The C.E.O of GILEADBALM GROUP Whose Products And Services Span Different Sectors: Information Technology, Telecom, Marketing, Consulting, Real Estate, Oil And Gas, Agriculture, Etc. He Is Also The President And Founder Of INFINITY FOUNDATION, An NGO That Helps Orphans And Less Privileged Children.

Infinity Foundation Has Impacted Over 2000 Orphans And Street Children In Africa; With Chapters Spread Across Different Tertiary

Institutions In Nigeria And Expanding To Other Schools Across The Globe.

The Foundation Also Hosts The Infinity Foundation Charity Award (IFCA), An Individual And Corporate Social Responsibility Award Program.

A Graduate Of Microbiology From Olabisi Onabanjo University, And Member Of The Institute Of Strategic Management, He Is Highly Sought After On TV And Radio.

Having A Vision Of Helping In The Establishment And Growth Of Youths In Every Area Of Their Lives, Stephen Has A Strong Passion To See Undergraduates And Graduates Come Up With Ideas That Will Cause A Business Revolution In Nigeria And AFRICA. His Mentorship Platform Has Helped Thousands In The Area Of Business.

A Relationship Expert And Exceptional Writer, Stephen Akintayo Is Author To Several Bestselling Books Which Include The Mobile Millionaire; Indestructible: Turning Your Mess

To Your Message; Soulmates; And Survival Instinct.

He Is An Ordained Pastor With Living Faith Church Worldwide, And Is Happily Married With Two Sons.

## CONTACT
Telephone:
(+234) 818 662 7339, 803 942 4917

BBPIN:
29B3B350

Facebook:
www.facebook.com/stephenakintayong

Twitter:
www.twitter.com/stephenakintayo

Skype:
stephenakintayo

Websites:
stephenakintayo.com;

http://gtext.com.ng;
http://infinityfoundation.org.ng

Email:
info@stephenakintayo.com;
Stephenakintayo@gmail.com